THE WEL

JOAN PE

Welsh translation by Delyth Evans

Dolls dressed by Mary Hannah Dolls
Photographs by Michael Corrin
Illustrations by Allison Fewtrell

Domino Books Ltd.
P O Box 78,
Swansea SA1 1YT

DOMINO

ISBN 1 85122 088 7

ISBN 1 855122 093 3 *Y Ddoli Gymreig*

FOREWORD

Although the Welsh doll and Welsh costume are unique to the Principality, surprisingly little has been written about them. Available in Welsh and English, this book shows how the Welsh doll today was preceded by numerous dolls from all parts of Wales and the national costumed doll evolved after a long period of time. The Welsh doll is put in perspective, showing how it fits into those items collectable and cherished by young and old.

I should like to thank Delyth Evans for her translation work, Denise Quick of Mary Hannah Dolls for the way in which she dressed the dolls, Michael Corrin for capturing the appeal of the dolls in his photographs and Allison Fewtrell for the line illustrations.

EJP

January, 1990

Covers
On the front cover is doll number 15 dressed in the traditional St. David's Day costume worn in Wales today.
On the back cover is doll number 12 dressed in 19th. century Welsh fashion of nursing a baby.

CONTENTS

From the same publishers:
Welsh Doll Postcards
Welsh Dolls Colouring Book

THE WELSH DOLL
IN HISTORY

The word *doll* (*cf. daul* Norse, *doche* old German, *pupa* Latin) describes an effigy modelled, however crudely, on the human form. The earliest examples were replicas or symbols of departed spirits. Dolls from 3000 - 2000 BC, carved of flat pieces of wood, geometrically painted and with hair made of strings of clay or wood, have been found in Egyptian graves. Ancient Greek dolls have also survived with arms and legs secured to their bodies with metal pins.

There have been many suggestions about how the word *doll* evolved. Some say that it is a shortened form of *Dorothea* or *Dorothy*. Others argue that it stems from *idol*. In any event, the *Oxford Dictionary of Christian Names* suggests that the word was not used as a description of a toy until 1700. In the Middle Ages, clay dolls were popular. They had a circular depression in their breasts and it is thought that godparents put a coin in this hole and gave the doll as a first gift to their godchild when he or she was baptised.

Later, dolls were used to model clothes in days when photography, fashion books and live models were non-existent. In 1391, for example, the Queen of England sent for a set of dolls from France which showed her what the clothes in the French court were like. Her dressmakers could then copy the designs. This practice continued into the 18th. century. When they were finished with, it was customary to give these fashion dolls to young daughters.

Up to the 18th. century, dolls were called *babies* or *little ladies* and wore grown up clothes: replicas of adults as it were. The English word *puppet*, the French *poupée*, the German *puppe* and the Dutch *pop* all stem from the Latin *pupa*, a girl, but there were and are, of course, boy as well as girl dolls.

Dolls have been made from almost every imaginable material: bark, birch, bone, breadcrumbs, cardboard, clay, cones, grass, gingerbread, leather, moss, paper, papier mâché, rag, seed pods, terra cotta, tin, wood and even crystallised fruit. They have been stuffed with bran, cork, corn, cotton batting, crumpled paper, down, feathers, grass, hay, horsehair, sand, sawdust, straw and at one time live birds were used instead of stuffing to give them the appearance of being alive.

Throughout history, dolls have followed closely the fashions of the times. When crinolines were in vogue, dolls wore crinolines; when bustles were fashionable, they wore bustles. Welsh dolls were no exception. The Principality had local fashions which varied according to time and place. Welsh dolls often reflected a particular custom, occupation, trade or profession. Such occupations included sheepminding and sheep rearing, dairy work, fishing, spinning, prawn, shrimp- or cockle-gathering, market trading and mining. Thus, there were particular dolls for different parts of Wales often suited to the work people did: copper mining in Anglesey, cockle-gathering in Penclawdd, fishing in Pembrokeshire, spinning in Breconshire and so on.

What is regarded today as the Welsh national costume, finally emerged in the 19th. century. This was based on peasant costume with the characteristics somewhat exaggerated. A general feeling was encouraged that everything in Wales: costumes, dolls, furniture, crafts, lovespoons, weddings, funerals were all different from elsewhere and worth preserving. The newly born tourist business fostered this outlook. A typical Welsh doll was needed and a cottage industry was born.

THE WELSH DOLL
AND NATIONAL COSTUME

The emergence of the traditional Welsh doll is closely linked with the history of Welsh national costume. Before the 19th. century, there was no truly *national* costume but gradually over a period of a hundred years, a typical costume became established. Even this had local variations but by the latter part of the century, dolls were dressed in this identifiable costume.

The traditional Welsh doll is dressed in a combination of the following:

The underskirt or petticoat.	Apron.
Bloomers.	Shawl.
The gown or betgwn.	The white cap.
Fichu.	The hat.
Whittle.	Stockings.
Cloak.	Shoes.

The Underskirt or Petticoat
The word *petticoat* comes from the old French *petite cote* and was originally a man's undershirt. By the Middle Ages, it had become a woman's undergarment tied around the waist with ribbons or tapes. In the 1860s, support for the Italian liberator, Garibaldi's *redshirts* created a fashion for red and in this case, red flannel petticoats.

Traditionally, the Welsh petticoat varied little in style or cut and was fairly full and ankle length. Two or three tucks were added at the bottom and the hem was usually deep and sometimes braid was added to stiffen it. The most popular colour was red, scarlet or crimson and the basic fabric used was Welsh homespun cloth or flannel. In some dolls, the homespun produced was greyish, oatmeal or light with little colour whilst flannel was white, cream, grey or even light blue. In later dolls, home-made cloth and patterns were replaced by machine-made cotton material and these are used to dress many dolls today.

Bloomers

In the middle of the 19th. century, Dexter Bloomer, editor of the New York journal, *The Seneca County Courier*, published an article suggesting that the short skirts and ankle-length trousers worn by Turkish women were far more practical than the long petticoats worn in America, Europe and elsewhere. Mr. Bloomer's wife, Amelia, then advocated more functional clothing for women, especially in her own feminist paper, *The Lily*. By the 1880s and 1890s bloomers had become popular attire.

As far as Welsh dolls were concerned, flannel or homespun was used for this undergarment in dolls of the late 19th. century. These were replaced by cotton in later dolls. Bloomers were gathered towards the ankle by cord (and later elastic) and in early dolls were hidden from sight by the underskirt or petticoat. Welsh dolls today often have bloomers which are a feature of their dress and are not hidden.

The Gown or Bedgown (Betgwn)

This was a loose upper garment worn over a petticoat by the peasant classes in the North of England and in Europe. The gown was usually made of woollen material in one colour or with vertical stripes of black or two contrasting colours.

Some dolls have gowns which are long and full with two wide pleats at the back. Others have those which resemble short blouses: the sleeves of these gowns are short. Sometimes they have detachable pieces of black alpaca fitted at the elbow with bows of black ribbon which show that they could be tied to the gown. This doll outfit follows the practice of a working girl, for after the dirty work of the day was finished, she could attach these pieces making elegant full length sleeves to the gown for 'walking out'.

Fichu

This was a 19th. century garment consisting of a small scarf or shawl. It was worn draped around the shoulders and often fastened with a brooch at the breast. A fichu can also mean a ruffle or a piece of fabric sewn across the bosom of a gown or dress.

In Welsh dolls, this is often made of white linen and placed around the neck. It may also be checked or striped and is often replaced by a shawl.

Whittle

This garment was probably Flemish in origin and consisted of a rectangular piece of cloth worn over the shoulders. It is sometimes used on dolls instead of the more traditional shawl. Often red in colour, it is usually made of Welsh wool.

Cloak

This is the generic term for a loose outer garment, which may have sleeves or not. It covers the body from the shoulders to hips, knees or ankles and may be with or without a collar. It was designed for walking particularly in cold weather and was later superseded by the winter coat or overcoat.

For the Welsh doll, the cloak falls from the shoulders to below the knees and it can be red, green, blue or grey. It may cover the whole costume and often has a gathered hood.

Apron

The apron became fashionable in the latter part of the 19th. century and beautifully embroidered aprons were used on 19th. century dolls. They were often made of flannel and today traditional dolls have flannel aprons in black and white stripes or checks often finished with lace embroidered edges. White cotton material is also used.

Shawl

The first shawls reached Europe in the 18th. century when British and French soldiers returned from war in India. The patterns and designs were influenced by these Indian versions. Early 18th. century shawls were small squares but eventually they developed to cover most of the upper body. The Welsh doll wears a shawl that may be draped or folded over the shoulders. Some are patterned and the cloth may be fine or a heavier Welsh homespun. The favourite colour is red or scarlett sometimes with a black check.

White cap and hat of the traditional St. David's Day costume.

The White Cap

This was a frilled close-fitting cap or kerchief worn on the head. Normally worn indoors, it fitted under a hat outdoors and was often trimmed with ribbon bows and strings.

Sometimes dolls are dressed in this simple cap without a hat but more traditionally, the cap made of white cotton or cambric covers the ears and is tied by a bow under the chin: it sets off the Welsh hat.

The Welsh Hat

There have always been hats or hoods of one type or another. The Egyptians used heavy wigs to shield their heads from the sun and the turban, fez and burnous were all used by early Mediterranean peoples. By mediaeval times, the veil and capuchon were in use and women also wore the wimple, a cloth draped round the head and neck and covering the chin.

The origin of the tall or beaver hat worn in Wales has been discussed for many years. Lord Raglan suggested the fashion came from the English gentry of the 17th. century. However, in the 18th. century, ladies in the French court wore high hats and a hat in Carmarthen museum names the maker as *André,* a Parisian designer. William Coxe travelling in Monmouthshire in 1801 noted:

The women were mostly wrapped in long cloth cloaks of a dark blue or brown colour: all of them wore mob caps neatly plaited over the forehead and ears and tied above the chin, several had also round felt hats like those worn by the men, or large chip hats covered with black silk and fastened under the chin.[1]

Later in the century, Benjamin Heath Malkin wrote:

The dress in Glamorganshire is not so strongly marked as in most other countries except that the women universally adopt the man's hat: but they wear it with a very good grace.[2]

[1] *An Historical Tour in Monmouthshire*
[2] *The Scenery . . . of South Wales*

Doll number 2 dressed in 18th. century working clothes.

Dr Ilid Anthony of the Welsh Folk Museum has stated:

In all illustrations of the Welsh lady of the 18th. century, the beaver hat had a wide brim, but the crown was no higher than that of a man's top hat and *the hat developed to be the most characteristic feature of the Welsh lady's costume when the height of the crown was extended upwards.*[4]

During the mid-Victorian period, the height of the crown of the hats increased almost every year. It seems clear that the tall Welsh hat was a 19th. century development.

It is this hat which is the most familiar feature of Welsh dolls and since the late 19th. century, they have been dressed in black hats with crowns from 1 to 4 inches high (depending on the size of the doll) and made of felt, covered with silk. The hat is worn over the white mob cap.

Stockings
In Wales, stockings were generally hand knitted and were white, grey or black. Those without soles were kept in place by loops of wool round the big toe. In older Welsh dolls the stockings are made of flannel or wool. Contemporary dolls have white cotton stockings which contrast with their black shoes.

Shoes
Soft shoes were in use some 30,000 years ago as a means of protecting the foot from injury but the modern shoe developed from the 17th. century. Cromwell's armies needed reliable footwear and strong leather soles were made.

Some Welsh dolls have no shoes, harking back to when Welsh peasants had none either. Some wear clogs as did working class people but most contemporary dolls are dressed in black, patent-type, flat, slipper-like shoes with no laces.

[4]*The Welsh Costume,* published by the National Federation of Women's Institutes.

Doll number 1 dressed in eighteenth century village clothes.

TYPES OF WELSH DOLL

This section considers the main types of Welsh doll in terms of the materials used and the variations in different parts of the Principality. The dolls featured in the illustrations have been specially dressed by one of the most skilful doll makers in Wales, Denise Quick of Mary Hannah Dolls, Carmarthen.

1. Doll dressed in 18th. century village clothes. (Radnor)

White underskirt, grey petticoat, black and grey striped betgwn, red and black striped apron, white lace collar, large red whittle or shawl, white bonnet, black, shallow felt hat, black shoes.

2. Doll dressed in 18th. century country working clothes. (Caernarfonshire)

White petticoat, grey flannel tucked underskirt, black and white checked apron, purple betgwn, white lace collar, brown and cream checked shawl, white overarm, white bonnet, black felt hat tied with red ribbon, basket of flowers.

3. Doll dressed in 18th. century costume as worn by Mary Jones. (Bala)

White petticoat, red and white striped skirt, black and red checked short betgwn, black turnover, white bonnet, straw hat with black band, holding a bible. (It is thought that the black felt bag carried by Mary Jones may have contained her shoes since most of the time she walked barefoot.)

4. Doll dressed in 18th. century village clothes. (Denbigh)

White underskirt, brown petticoat, green bedgown (betgwn), cream flannel apron, white bonnet, brown felt hat, black shoes.

Dolls dressed in eighteenth century costumes.

| 2 | 4 | 3 |
| 5 | 6 | |

Dolls dressed in nineteenth century costumes.

10	8	13
9	14	

5. Doll dressed in 18th. century upper class bridal wear. (Carmarthenshire)

White underskirt, cream silk petticoat (quilted), silk gown, black shoes.

6. Doll dressed in 18th. century village fisherwoman's bridal wear. (Rhyl)

White underskirt, blue flannel dress (quilted), black felt fitted jacket pleated at the back, white lace collar, large blue and black striped shawl, black straw hat with blue ribbon, white bonnet, black shoes.

7. Doll dressed in 19th. century cocklewoman's clothes. (Glamorgan)

White underskirt, rust petticoat, brown striped apron, dark brown betgwn pinned at back, white lace collar, white lace bonnet, black bonnet with thick pad or dorch, black shoes, cockle basket.

8. Doll dressed in 19th. century village clothes. (Montgomery)

White underskirt, black petticoat, black and green betgwn pinned at the back, white apron, white lace collar, white bonnet, black beaver hat, black shoes.

9. Doll dressed in 19th. century mining working clothes. (Anglesey)

White petticoat, heavy brown flannel dress, fawn apron, fawn checked turnover, flat brown felt hat.

10. Doll dressed in 19th. century peasant clothes. (Cardiganshire)

White underskirt, maroon and blue checked flannel dress, grey flannel apron (tucked), red and blue checked shawl or turnover, white bonnet, tall beaver hat, black shoes.

11. Doll dressed in 19th. century dairymaid's clothes. (Monmouth)

White underskirt, purple petticoat, blue and red striped betgwn, brown flannel apron, white lace collar, white bonnet, straw hat with flowers, black shoes.

Dolls dressed in nineteenth century costumes.

12. Doll dressed in 19th. century Welsh fashion of nursing a baby. (Merionethshire)

White underskirt, purple petticoat, blue betgwn pinned at the back, maroon and blue large nursing shawl, white apron, white lace bonnet, black beaver hat, black shoes, basket. Baby in white nursing wrap and bonnet.

13. Doll dressed in 19th. century fisherwoman's clothes. (Pembroke)

White underskirt, grey flannel petticoat (tucked), patterned blouse, grey and black striped apron, grey mix shawl (turnover), patterned kerchief, black felt hat, black shoes, cane basket with leather strap.

14. Doll dressed in 19th. century woollen spinner's clothes. (Breconshire)

White underskirt, red petticoat, black and white checked tucked apron, black and grey striped betgwn pinned at the back, red shawl or white fold over shoulder, white bonnet, black beaver hat, black shoes, home spun wool tied across front, basket of carded wool.

15. Doll dressed in traditional St. David's Day costume. (Wales today)

White underskirt, red petticoat with black stripe at the bottom, black and white striped apron, black and red striped betgwn pinned at back, red, black and white striped shawl, white lace bonnet, black beaver hat, black shoes.

Wooden dolls have been made in the Principality for centuries. The best known firm still involved in using this material is Worldwide Artistic Products, Welsh Craft Workshop, Llangollen Road, Acrefair, Wrexham, Clwyd. (At one time, they specialised in beautifully made peg dolls.) Their latest range has wooden heads with hand-painted faces. Dressed in Welsh flannel, this doll has been sold from Anchorage in Alaska to Stanley in the Falklands and has recently been bought by the Epcot Centre, Disney World, Florida.

Papier mâché, composition or *plastic dolls* are available in Wales and come from a variety of sources. These

Doll number 9 dressed in nineteenth century mining working clothes.

are then dressed in the Principality in genuine Welsh materials. Manufacturers are careful to distinguish between 'dolls made in Wales' and 'dolls dressed in Wales'.

For a doll made completely in Wales, there are the delightful, *handmade, rag dolls* made by Denise Quick of Mary Hannah Dolls. Denise works at home in her cottage in the Towy valley, near Llandeilo. All the flannel comes from a local woollen mill and the wool used for the hair in some of the dolls is hand spun by Denise. Her two young daughters, Anna and Sian, help when needed. The dolls appeal to a wide range of people, from children to collectors. They have been exported to the USA, Australia and Japan and have been exhibited at the Welsh Office, the House of Commons and for the Princess of Wales at Kensington Palace. Denise numbers each doll and keeps a record of each sale.

Porcelain (glazed porcelain), parian (white bisque) and bisque (unglazed porcelain) are all types of ceramics used to make dolls, especially their heads. Few doll manufacturers work with these materials but there are several specialising in porcelain and bisque figurines: Welsh dolls in national costume as well as dragons, cocklewomen, coracle fishermen, lovespoon carvers and many others make delightful subjects.

Pictures of Welsh dolls are used in a variety of ways and on a variety of materials, Welsh slate being one of the most popular and enduring.

Finally, there are the Maesyfed Mice by Maesyfed Mice Creations Ltd., Bwthyn Draenog, Walton, Presteign, Powys. These depict an imagined community of mice living in a small town set within a remote Mid Wales valley in the year 1860. Beautifully made, dressed in traditional Welsh costume, the mice come to life in the little books that relate their everyday adventures.

Doll number 8 dressed in nineteenth century village clothes.

A WELSH DOLL GLOSSARY

Alice band: narrow ribbon or velvet worn across the top of the head to keep hair off the forehead. Named after the heroine in Lewis Carroll's *Through the Looking Glass* (1872).

Ankle strap: material or elastic worn as decoration and as a device for securing the shoe to the foot.

Antique doll: describes a doll over 75 years old.

Applied ears: describes ears attached after the head of a doll has been moulded.

Apron: a small piece of cloth worn in front to protect clothes and tied at the back of the waist with strings made of the same material as the apron. Most Welsh dolls wear aprons.

Bald head: a doll which has no cut-away crown.

Balloon sleeve: 19th. century sleeve shape that was full over the upper arm and narrowed from the elbow to the wrist.

Beaver hat: the traditional headgear of contemporary Welsh dolls. The tall hat, copied from man's attire, came to be regarded as an essential element of the dress of Welsh dolls from the beginning of the 20th. century.

Belton-type doll: describes a doll with a head without a cut-away crown. It has a number of holes to which the wig could be attached.

Bedgown: see gown.

Betgwn: see gown.

Bergère: a straw hat with a low crown and wide brim, first popular in the 18th. century.

Bishop sleeve: a long sleeve on a dress or blouse which is full below the elbow and is gathered or loose at the wrist.

Bisque: an unglazed, matt-surface ceramic used in making dolls. It is usually poured into a mould or pressed before being fired.

Bloomers: since the late 19th. century, has been used to denote any loose, full undergarment. They were worn under long skirts and gathered between the knee and ankle. They appear on Welsh dolls from the 1850s onwards.

Bonnet: headgear with or without a front brim which covered the top, sides and back of the head and was tied under the chin. Used on dolls in many parts of Wales, particularly before the tall beaver hat became fashionable.

Bonnet head: a doll with a hat or bonnet moulded on to the head. This was sometimes done in Wales because the tall hat was likely to fall off.

Broadcloth: generic term for a variety of material. Originally, it was a woollen shirting fabric cut wider than other cloth.

Cape: outer garment which is a shorter version of the cloak (see below) but without slits for arms.

Cardigan: long-sleeved jacket of knitted worsted which is buttoned down the front. Such a jacket was first worn by British army officers during the Crimean War and named after the 7th. Earl of Cardigan, James Thomas Brudenell (1797 - 1868), who led the charge of the Light Brigade.

Character doll: a type of doll modelled on children and babies in the last century. Many Welsh dolls are of this type and are given traditional names such as Myfanwy, Blodwen and Megan.

Check: pattern of criss crossing lines of one or more colours on cloth. Developed in Scotland during the 19th. century as an alternative to tartan. In Wales checks were adapted by weavers to produce local patterns based on tartan patterns and colours.

Chignon: A type of hairstyle often used on Welsh dolls. A popular style from the 19th. century, created by coiling long hair into a loose, but carefully pinned bun at the back of the head.

China head doll: a doll which has a head made of glazed porcelain. This ceramic material was widely used until replaced by bisque in the second part of the 19th. century. (see bisque)

Cloak: Loose garment with or without sleeves worn over a dress or costume. It covers the body from the shoulders to the hips, knees or ankles.

Clogs: Wooden shoes worn by working girls in many parts of Wales in the 19th. century. Some Welsh dolls wear clogs and recall this tradition.

Composition: Name given to a variety of materials used in making the bodies of dolls such as wood pulp, sawdust or papier mâché.

Contemporary: describes the clothes, accessories and equipment of the same period as a particular doll.

Corsage: small bouquet of flowers worn at the waist or bosom of dresses during the 19th. century. A Welsh doll may wear daffodils.

Cotton: material used to make dolls' clothes, especially underwear. In modern Welsh dolls, it often replaces flannel.

Crochet: decorative craftwork made by looping yarn or thread with a crochet hook. Often used to decorate shawls.

Cummerband: a wide cloth band worn as a sash around the waist. The word comes from the Hindi and Persian *kamarband* meaning *loincloth.*

Dart: pointed tuck in a garment to shape it to a doll's body.

Elastic: fabric made from the interwoven threads of india rubber. Often used in doll's underwear.

Embroidery: ornamental needlework usually with coloured designs to decorate a fabric.

Ethnic:	describes garments inspired by clothes indigenous to some country or area.
Fashion doll:	(a) a doll used to exhibit the types of clothes worn at a particular time and place. They were used to show samples of the kind of clothes worn. (b) describes bisque head dolls with shaped bodies dressed in fashionable clothes popular in the late 19th. century.
Felspar:	white coloured mineral used to produce a non-translucent paste used in doll manufacture.
Fichu:	small scarf or shawl worn draped around the shoulders. Often fastened with a brooch at the bosom.
Flannel:	generic term for woollen fabrics woven in different weights of worsted. Usually soft, it is made of a plain or twilled weave slightly napped on one side. In the 19th. century it was often used for petticoats and dolls dressed in this fabric are still popular today.
Flange neck:	describes a joint which allows a doll's head to move from side to side.
Frill:	narrow ruffle gathered to the edge of a neckline, armhole, cuff or hem.
French slope:	describes a steeply cut-away crown which usually has a cork pate.
'Frozen Charlotte':	name often given to a doll made in one piece with the head, torso, arms and legs moulded together. Also called bathing babies, pillar dolls and solid chinas.
Godet:	piece of triangular shaped fabric which is wider at the bottom than the top. It is sewn into a skirt, dress or coat to increase fullness.
Gown: **(Also bedgown/ betgwn)**	Traditional garment made of thick flannel worn by young and old over the petticoat. Often red in colour, it has been worn by Welsh dolls for centuries.

Gusset: small, triangular piece of fabric inserted in the seams of a garment to increase its strength or to enlarge it.

Hoof feet: describes the carved feet of early wooden dolls which did not distinguish the toes.

Intaglio eyes: painted eyes which have the details of iris and pupil engraved on them.

Jabot: decorative frill of lace pinned at the base of the neck or breast.

Jointed body: describes a doll with joints at the wrist, shoulder, hips, knees, ankles and waist enabling parts of its body to be moved independently.

Knife pleats: narrow pleats which when pressed form regular, sharp edges on a skirt or dress.

Lambswool: wool from young sheep often used to make small garments for dolls.

Leg-of-mutton sleeve: sleeve which is tight-fitting from the wrist to elbow and balloons out from the elbow to the shoulder.

Linen: fabric made from flax fibre and which is used to manufacture fine or coarse cloth. Often used to make dolls' underwear.

Mantle: hooded cloak worn as an outer garment in the mid and late 19th. century.

Mitten hands: doll's hands with fingers closed and only the thumb separate.

'Monkey' feet: doll's feet with separate toes.

Moulded teeth: doll's teeth that have been moulded at the same time as the head.

Myfanwy Jones: Welsh cut out doll with this name was made by Margaret Holgate as a souvenir of the 1969 Investiture of HRH the Prince of Wales.

Open/closed mouth:	refers to a doll which appears to have its lips parted (although there is no actual opening). White paint is often applied between the lips to give this affect.
Pagoda sleeve:	three quarter or half length sleeve which was frilled to the elbow where it became wider with several tiers or flounces.
Paperweight eyes:	a doll's glass eyes with fine white lines drawn through the iris. This gives added colour depth and makes them more luminous. Viewed from the side, they appear to curve outwards.
Papier mâché:	a paper pulp which, with added whitener and the use of glue, was used to make dolls' heads and torsos in the early 19th. century. By the end of the century, the process had so improved that the papier mâché could be poured into moulds - this increased the numbers of dolls that could be made.
Parian:	a pure white bisque used for making dolls. The features were usually painted on this material.
Patchwork:	a doll made by sewing small pieces of different materials together.
Peasant:	style of clothes that refers to the rural costumes of a particular country.
Peter Pan collar:	flat, round collar about 2 inches deep, sometimes heavily starched. Named after Peter Pan, the boy hero of J M Barrie's play and book.
Petticoat:	a type of underskirt tied around the waist with ribbons or tapes. Throughout the 19th. century it was made of various fabrics including linen, cotton or muslin. It is an essential part of a Welsh doll's costume.
Pinafore:	type of apron with a bib front, a halter neck and a long skirt that ties behind the waist.
Plaid:	tartan or check cloth.

Porcelain: synonym for china in relation to the material used to make a doll's head.

Portrait doll: doll modelled on a famous person.

Poured wax: describes dolls made by wax being poured directly into a mould.

Provenance: a document which gives details of a doll's history. It is passed on to subsequent owners after an owner's death.

Puff sleeves: short sleeves which are gathered and set into the shoulders of garments to create a puffed effect.

Pumps: lightweight, flat, plain shoes which used to be worn by 18th. century servants. These, in black, are the usual shoes for Welsh dolls.

Quilting: Cotton filling enclosed by two layers of fabric held together by stitching to form a raised pattern.

Rag dolls: dolls made with fabric only. Have been made for centuries in the Principality often with Welsh wool stuffing and dressed in Welsh flannel.

Raglan: sleeve extending from the neckline to the wrist. Named after Lord Raglan (1788 - 1855), British Commander during the Crimean War.

Shawl: a square or rectangular piece of cloth worn loosely around the shoulders and loosely tied in front over the bust. The first shawls reached Wales in the 18th. century with British soldiers returning from fighting in India and Europe. The traditional Welsh doll invariably wears a shawl. (See 'Welsh fashion')

Shift: early 19th. century garment shaped like a nightgown and usually made of white linen. A chemise, it was quickly adopted by those who worked on the land.

Shoes: Welsh dolls traditionally wear black, flat shoes which contrast with their white socks.

Shoulder-head: head of a doll which has its head and shoulders moulded in one piece.

Smock: in mediaeval times, this was a loose, knee or calf length garment with a yoke. It was made of cotton or linen and worn by women under their gowns.

Spoon-hands: the hands on a doll which only have the thumbs formed.

Stockings: dolls traditionally wear white stockings under their Welsh costume.

Tapestry: ornamental woven cloth in which the design tells a story.

Tartan: closely woven woollen cloth which originated in Scotland. Different patterns identified individual clans. Tartan patterns are sometimes used for shawls on Welsh dolls.

Tinted bisque: describes dolls with moulded hair that are made of bisque that is paler than flesh-coloured bisque. (See bisque.)

Twill: fabric woven with diagonal lines of weft thread which pass under and over the warp threads.

Wash over eye: a deep pink coloration applied between eyelid and the forehead to give depth to a doll's features.

Wax-over: denotes a doll made from a composition which is dipped into molten wax or on which molten wax has been applied.

Welsh fashion: refers to the particular way a baby is carried in Wales. The shawl is large and wrapped around the mother and the baby. Welsh dolls often show this way of nursing infants.

Dolls and Dolls' Customs Elsewhere

Aristocrat doll: a type of doll made at the time of the French revolution. The doll's head was detachable so that it could easily come off!

Doll festival: Japanese boys have an annual doll festival from the first of May after they are born until their 15th. birthday.

Dresden doll: doll with a glazed porcelain head which first became popular in the early 19th. century. Now regarded as collectors' items.

Fingo doll: in the Orange Free State, every girl is given a doll to keep for her first child. When the child is born, the mother receives a second doll to keep for the second child.

Friendship doll: a doll often given as a gift to a visitor to modern Japan.

Golden angel: a small doll sold in Nuremberg at Christmas time. Originated over 300 years ago when a young mother lost her daughter. Her husband, a toy maker, made a doll with his daughter's features and painted it gold to represent an angel. The wife realised her daughter was at peace and was comforted. Replicas of the doll still appear at Yuletide.

Jack-in-the-box: doll in a spring loaded box. Probably originated in the 13th. century from the idea of the devil being trapped in a box.

Kachina doll: doll used by Indians to represent the rainbow and used in their religous ceremonies. After use in this way, the doll was given to children. At annual Kachina ceremonies, the small figures were given to children by masked adults impersonating legendary, supernatural Kachina who took the people's prayers to the gods.

Matreshka dolls: traditional Russian wooden dolls which nest inside each other and represent five generations.

Queen Anne doll: wooden doll dating from the end of the 17th. to the early 18th. century and now collectors' items.

Scapegoat doll: doll formerly given to Japanese mothers to ward off evil spirits from their children.